D0856226

EXTREME WEATHER

Ice Storms

by Anne Wendorff

Consultant:
Mark Seeley, Ph.D.,
University of Minnesota Extension
Meteorologist and Climatologist,
Department of Soil, Water, and Climate,
St Paul, Minn.

BLASTOFF!
4
READERS

BELLWETHER MEDIA • MINNEAPOLIS, MN

Note to Librarians, Teachers, and Parents:

Blastoff! Readers are carefully developed by literacy experts and combine standards-based content with developmentally appropriate text.

Level 1 provides the most support through repetition of high-frequency words, light text, predictable sentence patterns, and strong visual support.

Level 2 offers early readers a bit more challenge through varied simple sentences, increased text load, and less repetition of high-frequency words.

Level 3 advances early-fluent readers toward fluency through increased text and concept load, less reliance on visuals, longer sentences, and more literary language.

Level 4 builds reading stamina by providing more text per page, increased use of punctuation, greater variation in sentence patterns, and increasingly challenging vocabulary.

Level 5 encourages children to move from "learning to read" to "reading to learn" by providing even more text, varied writing styles, and less familiar topics.

Whichever book is right for your reader, Blastoff! Readers are the perfect books to build confidence and encourage a love of reading that will last a lifetime!

This edition first published in 2009 by Bellwether Media.

No part of this publication may be reproduced in whole or in part without written permission of the publisher. For information regarding permission, write to Bellwether Media Inc., Attention: Permissions Department, Post Office Box 19349, Minneapolis, MN 55419.

Library of Congress Cataloging-in-Publication Data
Wendorff, Anne.
  Ice storms / by Anne Wendorff.
    p. cm. – (Blastoff! readers. Extreme weather)
  Summary: "Simple text and full color photographs introduce beginning readers to the characteristics of ice storms. Developed by literacy experts for students in kindergarten through third grade"–Provided by publisher.
  Includes bibliographical references and index.
  ISBN-13: 978-1-60014-186-7 (hardcover : alk. paper)
  ISBN-10: 1-60014-186-2 (hardcover : alk. paper)
  1. Ice storms–Juvenile literature. I. Title.

  QC926.37.W46 2009
  551.55'6–dc22   2008015219

Contents

What Is an Ice Storm?

Have you ever seen rain fall on a cold winter day? The rain may freeze as soon as it hits the ground or objects near the ground.

Freezing rain forms an ice layer that can cover everything in sight. A storm that brings freezing rain is called an ice storm.

Ice Storms and Their Effects

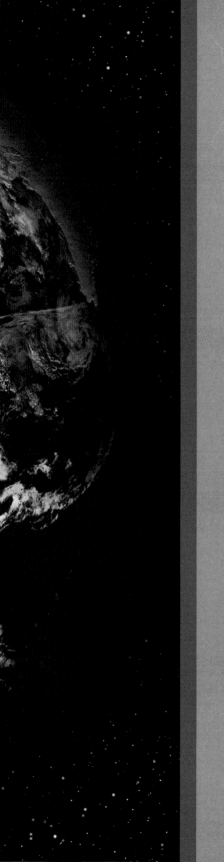

Ice storms form when cold air and warm air meet in a certain way. Air is always moving over the surface of the earth. A large area of air with the same temperature is called an **air mass**. The sun heats some air masses more than others. In winter, some air masses can be very cold.

Air masses can form layers. Ice storms
happen when there are several layers.
For example, a layer of very cold air
high in the sky may cover a layer of
warmer air.

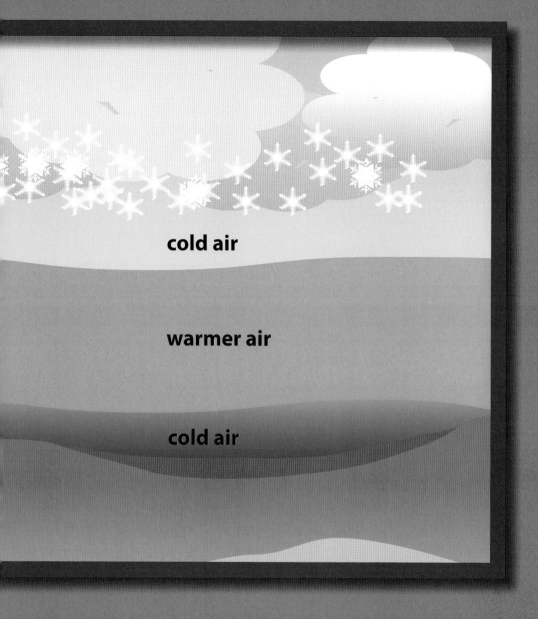

cold air

warmer air

cold air

The warmer air may then cover another layer of cold air near the ground. This cold air must be below 32 degrees **Fahrenheit** (0 degrees **Celsius**). That is the temperature at which water freezes into ice.

In an ice storm, snow forms in the highest cold air mass. It then falls out of this cold air and into the layer of warmer air below. The warmer air melts the snow into rain.

cold air

warmer air

cold air

The cold layer near the ground cools the rain. Finally, the rain freezes when it hits the cold ground or objects near the ground.

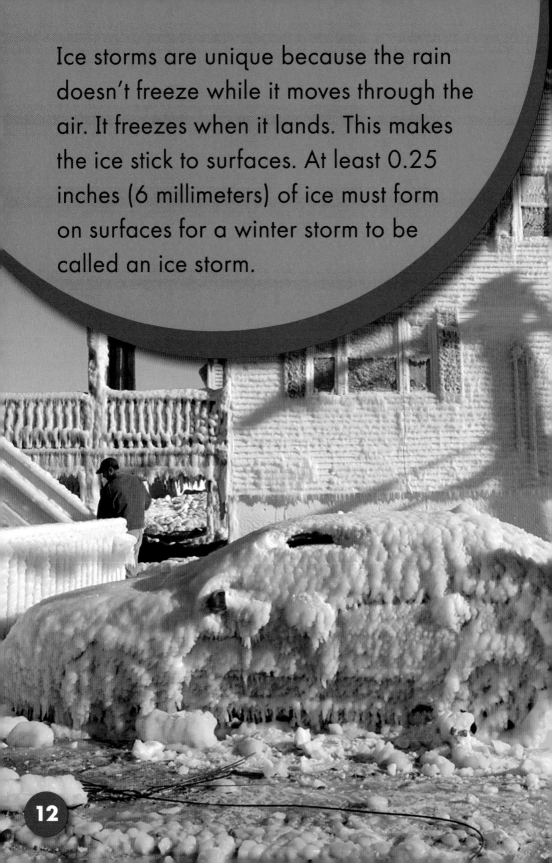

Ice storms are unique because the rain doesn't freeze while it moves through the air. It freezes when it lands. This makes the ice stick to surfaces. At least 0.25 inches (6 millimeters) of ice must form on surfaces for a winter storm to be called an ice storm.

Rain that freezes while it moves through the air forms **sleet** or **hail**. These can make a mess, but they don't stick to surfaces like freezing rain does. Sleet and hail can fall along with freezing rain before, during, and after an ice storm.

Ice storms can be very dangerous. Even
a thin layer of ice can make sidewalks
and roads extremely slippery. This makes
traveling difficult.

Heavy ice can break power lines. Tree branches and trunks can snap. The weight of ice can even cause the roofs of buildings to collapse.

CAUTION ROADS
MAY BE ICY

Predicting Ice Storms

Meteorologists try to predict ice storms. In winter, they look for the air mass layers that make an ice storm possible.

Meteorologists will issue an **ice storm warning** if they know conditions are right for an ice storm. This tells people to stay inside if possible, and to avoid travel. Unfortunately, ice storms can happen with little or no warning.

17

The Canadian Ice Storm of 1998

A severe ice storm hit Eastern Canada in January of 1998. Freezing rain covered the ground with 3 to 4 inches (8 to 10 centimeters) of ice.

The heavy ice broke power lines. Millions of people lost power. Some were trapped inside their houses for days.

fast fact

The Canadian Ice Storm caused over $5 billion in damage.

Rescue crews may have to wait for the ice storm to stop before going out to help people. Road crews put salt and sand on icy roads so vehicles can have a better grip.

Cleanup crews have a big job after an ice storm. They fix power lines, replace road signs, and pick up fallen tree branches. These crews help cities get up and running again after the damage of an ice storm.

Glossary

air mass—a very large section of air that moves over the surface of the earth; the air in one air mass is usually the same temperature.

Celsius—a system for measuring temperature; the Celsius system is used in most countries around the world.

Fahrenheit—a system for measuring temperature; the Fahrenheit system is used in the United States.

hail—small balls of ice that fall from the sky

ice storm warning—an announcement that an ice storm is coming

meteorologists—scientists who study weather

sleet—partly frozen rain

To Learn More

AT THE LIBRARY

Chambers, Catherine. *Big Freeze*. Chicago, Ill.: Heinemann, 2001.

Scheff, Duncan. *Ice and Hailstorms*. Chicago, Ill.: Raintree, 2001.

Temple, Bob. *Ice Storm! The 1998 Freeze*. New York: Bearport, 2006.

ON THE WEB
Learning more about
ice storms is as easy as 1, 2, 3.

1. Go to www.factsurfer.com

2. Enter "ice storms" into search box.

3. Click the "Surf" button and you will see a list of related web sites.

With factsurfer.com, finding more information is just a click away.

Index

The images in this book are reproduced through the courtesy of: Steven Senne / Associated Press, front cover, pp. 12-13; Getty Images, pp. 4-5; argus, pp. 6-7; Linda Clavel, pp. 8-9, 10-11; Baudy, p. 13 (inset); AFP / Getty Images, p. 14; Nati Harnik / Associated Press, p. 15; Javier Larrea / age fotostock, pp. 16-17; Jacques Boissinot / Associated Press, p. 18; Adrian Wyld / Associated Press, p. 19; Anton J. Geisser / age fotostock, p. 20; Larry W. Smith / Getty Images, p. 21.